BIG BEASTS

Lion

Stephanie Turnbull

Published by Saunders Book Company
27 Stewart Road, Collingwood, ON Canada L9Y 4M7

Designed by Hel James
Edited by Mary-Jane Wilkins

Library of Congress Cataloging-in-Publication Data
Turnbull, Stephanie.
  Lion / Stephanie Turnbull.
    pages cm. -- (Big beasts)
  Summary: "Describes the characteristics of Lions
and their life and habitats"-- Provided by publisher.
  Audience: K to Grade 3.
  Includes index.
  ISBN 978-1-77092-216-7 (paperback)
  1. Lion--Juvenile literature. I. Title.
  QL737.C23T87 2015
  599.757--dc23
                        2014003971

CIP record is available from Library and Archives Canada

Photo acknowledgements
l = left, r = right, t = top, b = bottom
title Eric Isselée/Shutterstock; page 3 Mogens Trolle/Shutterstock;
4 Villiers Steyn/Shutterstock; 5t iStockphoto/Thinkstock,
b hpbdesign/Shutterstock; 6 iStockphoto/Thinkstock;
8 iStockphoto/Thinkstock; 9 PETER HATCH/Shutterstock;
10 Alta Oosthuizen/Shutterstock; 13 StephenE/Shutterstock;
14 iStockphoto/Thinkstock; 15 moizhusein/Shutterstock;
16 Hemera/Thinkstock; 17 iStockphoto/Thinkstock;
18 PHOTOCREO Michal Bednarek/Shutterstock;
19 KA Photography KEVM111/Shutterstock; 20 iStockphoto/
Thinkstock; 21 Jupiterimages/Thinkstock; 22l Maggy Meyer/
Shutterstock, r iStockphoto/Thinkstock; 23 Joy Brown/
Shutterstock
Cover Eric Isselée/Shutterstock

Printed in China

DAD0059
032014
9 8 7 6 5 4 3 2 1

Contents

Lions are huge!

Tall and Strong

Lions are the tallest cats in the world. They are massive, muscular meat-eaters.

Thick, bushy manes help males look big and fierce.

A few lions have white fur.

Fierce Families

Most lions live on hot, dry grasslands in Africa. They stick together in big family groups called prides.

Each pride has a few lionesses, their cubs and one or two males.

Other lions are **not** welcome on their patch of land!

Lazy Days

It's far too **hot** for big, heavy lions to do much during the day. They rest and doze in the shade.

Sometimes lions stretch out in trees to catch a cool breeze and avoid irritating flies.

As the sun goes down, lions wake up. It's time to find food!

Excellent eyesight helps them spot prey in dim light.

When they see an antelope, zebra, or wildebeest, they crouch down and wait patiently for it to come near... then

pounce!

Big Eaters

Powerful lions can drag a big animal to the ground in a flash. They bite into its throat and hold on until it is dead.

Lions have 30 sharp teeth—perfect for ripping into flesh. They **eat** and **eat** until they are stuffed!

Smart Hunting

Lionesses move faster than males, so they make good hunters.

Sometimes they work together.

They form a sneaky circle around their prey... then *RUN* at it. The animal is trapped!

Everyone shares the feast afterwards.

15

Cute Cubs

Usually two or more cubs are born together.

They hide in bushes, drinking their mother's milk, until they are strong enough to join the pride.

Mothers carry cubs by holding the skin on their neck. It doesn't hurt them!

Growing Up

Cubs love to roll, tumble, and have play fights.

They grow strong and learn important hunting skills.

Mothers keep a careful watch for fierce hyenas and leopards who may try to catch and eat lion cubs.

Dinner Time

Lion Talk

Lions nuzzle each other and rub heads
to show they are friends.

If they think another lion wants to attack their pride, they snarl, hiss, and give a long, deep RROAAARRR that echoes for miles around.

This means "Stay away... or else!"

BIG Facts

Adult male lions may weigh more than ten big sacks of potatoes.

A lion can kill an antelope with one blow of its huge, heavy front paw.

Lions may attack animals as big as giraffes, but they have to be careful as a giraffe kick can kill!

A lion's long, wide tongue is covered in tiny hooks that help it scrape meat off bones.

Useful Words

lioness
A female lion. Lionesses are smaller than males.

mane
Thick hair around a male lion's head that darkens as he grows older.

prey
An animal that is hunted by another animal.

pride
A family group of lions living together.

Index

Web Link

Go to this web site for fantastic lion facts and photos:
www.nationalgeographic.com/kids/animals/creaturefeature/lion